NEW ENGLAND
Lighthouses

79 full-color pictures
Published by MEDS MAPS, Inc.
HARWICH, MA

NEW ENGLAND SEASHORE

MAINE

Eastport

Lubec

Machias

Bar Harbor

Camden

Rockland

AUGUSTA

Boothbay Harbor

Portland

NEW HAMPSHIRE

York

Kittery

PORTSMOUTH

Newburyport

Gloucester

BOSTON

MASSACHUSETTS

Provincetown

Plymouth

PROVIDENCE

Cape Cod

HARTFORD

RHODE ISLAND

CONNECTICUT

Newport

Nantucket

Mystic

New London

Martha's Vineyard

New Haven

Stonington

Mystic Seaport Lighthouse

This lighthouse marks the entrance to Mystic Seaport. The light is of similar design to Brant Point on Nantucket. Mystic Seaport is a living museum, comprised of many activities that one might find in a New England coastal village from the 1800's.   © Paul Montecalvo

Stonington Harbor Lighthouse

Stonington Harbor Lighthouse, built in 1824, was first located on Windmill Point guarding the west side of the harbor. Because of erosion, the government had the lighthouse torn down in 1840. A thirty-five foot stone tower with an attached dwelling replaced the original lighthouse. This time on the east side of the harbor. The lighthouse was discontinued in 1889 and today serves as a museum.

© Marjorie Monteleon

Five Mile Point Lighthouse

Five Mile Point Light, established in 1805, is one of the oldest in Connecticut. This lighthouse, first built of wood, was rebuilt of stone in 1840. This light guided ships to and from New Haven Harbor until the lighthouse was decommissioned in 1877. The lighthouse has been refurbished by the city and now serves as the chief attraction of the city's Lighthouse Park.

© William Johnson

Rhode Island Lights

Block Island- North Light was built in 1867, after earlier lights of 1829 and 1857 succumbed to the shifting sands of Sandy Point. The light was automated in 1955, operated until 1973, then replaced by an offshore beacon. A large preservation effort brought the lighthouse back to life in the spring of 1996. The original frensel lens was returned to the light tower and North Light was recommissioned as an active lighthouse, replacing the offshore beacon.

© Paul Rezendes

Block Island – North Light

Block Island – Southeast Light

Block Island-Southeast Light was built in 1873, and is the highest above sea level of any New England lighthouse. It features a magnificent first-order frensel lens built by the Henri LePaute Company of Paris for $10,000. The light flashes a unique green. The lighthouse was recently moved back from the eroding Mohegan Bluffs. The lighthouse is a massive Victorian brick structure constructed in Gothic Revival style.

© Marjorie Monteleon

Watch Hill Lighthouse

Watch Hill Light was built in 1808 and replaced in 1856 with the current granite block tower. A fourth order frensel lens is still active. The light is named after a watchtower that was erected on a hill during the King George's War in the 1740's. The watchtower was built to guard against naval attack.

© Marjorie Monteleon

Point Judith Lighthouse

Point Judith Light and Coast Guard Station guard the western entrance to the Narragansett Bay. The original wooden tower was built in 1810, but was blown over six years later. A replacement stone tower lasted until 1857, when the current octagonal tower was erected. The upper part of the tower is painted dark brown. This light guards the very dangerous coastal area known as the "graveyard of the Atlantic". Point Judith has threatened mariners with its shoals since European explorers first arrived. The point reaching several miles out into the Atlantic, is especially dangerous after a storm.

© Paul Rezendes

Rose Island Lighthouse

Rose Island Light was built in 1870 to guide ships around the shoals surronding Newport Harbor. The construction of the Newport Bridge in 1969 made this lighthouse obsolete. The bridge, towering above the lighthouse, is a more effective navigational marker. The light served until its deactivation in 1971. Rose Island Light has been restored and it is a bed and breakfast.

© Rose Island Lighthouse Foundation

Goat Island Light

Goat Island Light was first built in 1824 on the south end of Goat Island, guarding the entrance to Newport Harbor. The original light was replaced with a new light on the north end of the island in 1838. Construction of a new light and dwelling was approved in 1865. The keeper's house was rammed and destroyed by a submarine in 1922. The light, now automated, is still active.

© Marjorie Monteleon

Sakonnet Point Light

Sakonnet Point Light sits on a ledge at the mouth of the Sakonnet River. This light, built in 1884 is a caisson type design. The light ceased operation in 1954, and was sold to a private party in 1961. Donated to a preservation group in 1985, restoration is currently underway.

© Paul Rezendes

Beavertail Lighthouse

Beavertail Light sits on the tip of Conanicut Island in Beavertail State Park. Built in 1749 this is Rhode Island's first and America's third lighthose. The original tower burned a few years later and was replaced with a stone tower in 1753. Beavertail was important as a guide to shipping traffic bound for Newport, which was one of the busiest ports in the colonies. The current granite tower was built in 1856, closely resembling Watch Hill. A fourth order lens flashes a white signal.

© Marjorie Monteleon

Castle Hill Lighthouse

Castle Hill Light was built in 1890 to mark the eastern passage of Narragansett Bay. The 34 foot tower is constructed of granite blocks, with the upper part painted white. A small fifth-order frensel light flashes red.

© Marjorie Monteleon

Cape Cod Lights

Nobska Lighthouse

Nobska Light, built in 1828 and rebuilt in 1876, is perhaps the most picturesque lighthouse on Cape Cod. Nobska Light has a commanding position overlooking Falmouth and Woods Hole harbors.

© Jim Abts

The bluffs of Nobska provide a fine vantage point with the islands of Martha's Vineyard just across the narrows. The channel is one of the busiest sea traffic corners of the Cape. More than 30,000 vessels pass by annually. Its light flashes every 6 seconds and is visible 16 miles out to sea.

© Marjorie Monteleon

Chatham Lighthouse

Chatham Light was established in 1808 as Cape Cod's second lighthouse. It consisted of two brick towers and a keepers house. Later it was decided that Chatham's two lights were too costly to maintain. The north tower was moved in 1923 to Nauset Beach in Eastham, and the south tower was moved back from the bluff to it s present position next to the Chatham coast guard station, near the mouth of Chatham Harbor. It flashes its white light twice every ten seconds and can be seen up to 28 miles out to sea.

© Robert Dennis

Nauset Light

Nauset Light was built in 1877. The tower began service to mariners in Chatham as a sister light to the present Chatham Lighthouse. In 1923 the tower was dismanteled and moved to Eastham where it was rebuilt. The 48 foot, 100 ton Nauset Light flashes alternating red and white lights every ten seconds and is visible as far away as 23 miles out to sea. In November, 1996, through the efforts of the Nauset Light Preservation Society the tower and oil house were moved westward 323 feet back from the relentless surf of the North Atlantic.

© William Johnson
© Robert Dennis

Cape Cod Light

Cape Cod Light, located on a high bluff near Truro, was built in 1797, the first lighthouse on Cape Cod. Because of erosion, the lighthouse was replaced several times. The current structure was built in 1857. The light tower is fitted with a first-order Fresnel lens. One of only four working lighthouses on the Outer Cape, it was the last to become automated in 1986. At 120 feet above sea level, the lighthouse is aptly named Highland Light. In 1996, the 430 ton lighthouse was moved to a spot 553 feet inland. The coast continues to erode 2 to 3 feet per year.

Wood End Light

Wood End Light, built in 1872, the lighthouse is located between Race Point and Long Point and directly across from the harbor of Provincetown. Unlike other Cape lighthouses, Wood End Light is a square white tower and now powered by the sun.
It flashes a red light every ten seconds and has a range of 13 miles.

© William Johnson

Race Point Light

One of the worst stretches of land for shipwrecks along the entire Cape Cod coast is known as Race Point, but it was not until 1816 that the government built a lighthouse to protect mariners from the dreaded "Peaked Hill Bars". Between 1816 and 1846, more than 100 vessels were shipwrecked on the beach and offshore shoals. So treacherous is the area that Race Point Light is equipped with a foghorn to warn ships in poor visibility. The white light flashes every 10 seconds and can be seen 16 miles out to sea. The Keepers dwelling was recently completely restored.

© William Johnson

Long Point Light

At the inner extremity of the long streach of sandy terrain that curls up to a northernmost point well inside Provincetown Harbor, stands Long Point Light.
Built in 1827 and rebuilt in 1875, the light is now an unattended automatic station with a flashing green light. Its range is 8 miles out to sea.

© William Johnson

Three Sisters Light

Three 15 foot tall towers were built in 1838 and situated 150 feet apart close to the cliff's edge. Due to erosion, the lights were rebuilt several times. In 1911 the center light was again moved back from the cliffs and operated as a single light. The two other lights were sold. The remaining light ceased operation in 1923. The Cape Cod National Seashore has acquired all three lights and they have been restored and open to the public.

© Marjorie Monteleon

Stage Harbor Light

Stage Harbor Light is located on Harding Beach across from West Chatham. The light was built in 1880 and lost its lantern in the 1930's. The lighthouse is no longer in use.

© William Johnson

15

Martha's Vineyard Lights

The 51 foot red brick tower was built in 1856 to replace the wooden lighthouse that was built in 1799. This was the island's first lighthouse. This light marks the entrance to Vineyard Sound and guides ships away from the great reef of glacial boulders extending out from the cliffs for almost a mile. The colorful, varigated red clay cliffs that slope down to the ocean from the lighthouse cannot be rivaled anywhere else in New England. The light has alternating white and red flashes every 15 seconds and can be seen 24 miles out to sea.

© Jim Abts

Gay Head Light

Cape Pogue Light

The light was established on the northeast tip of Chappaquiddick Island, just east of Martha's Vineyard, in 1801. Erosion has caused the light to be replaced three times and moved several times. The current tower was constructed in 1893. The light flashes red every 4 seconds and is visible 9 miles out to sea.

© Paul Rezendes

East Chop Light

East Chop Light marks the eastern entrance of Vineyard Haven Harbor. A privately owned wooden beacon tower was built by Captain Silas Daggett in 1869. In 1875 the government purchased the lighthouse from a consortium of sea captains, then constructed the 40 foot tall cast iron conical tower that stands today. East Chop flashes its green light every 6 seconds and can be seen 9 miles out to sea.

© William Johnson

Edgartown Light

The first light was erected on the west side of the inner harbor at Edgartown in 1828. A hurricane destroyed the second light to stand on this site in 1938.
In 1941, the old Essex Light at Ipswich, Massachusetts was dismantled and shipped to Martha's Vineyard. This 45 foot tall tower is still in operation, fixed with a solar powered lens.Edgartown Light flashes its red light every six seconds and is visible 5 miles out to sea.

© William Johnson

West Chop Light

Chop is an Old-English term to describe the entrance of a harbor or channel. West Chop Light guards the entrance to Vineyard Haven Harbor. Built in 1817 with wood and rebuilt n 1838, the light has been moved back from eroding cliffs twice. The current 54 foot tower was built in 1891 and still operates today . The original 4th-order Fresnel optic flashes white every 4 seconds and can be seen 15 miles out to sea.

© Marjorie Monteleon

Great Point Light

Great Point Light, built in 1784, sits on the far northern tip of the island. The Great point light was visible 14 miles out to sea as a beacon to warn sailors or the treacherous Great Point Rip, shoals and currents that were the scene of 43 shipwrecks between 1863 and 1890. The original wooden tower was destroyed by fire in 1816. The following year a 70-foot tall stone tower was installed at Great Point and remained until a raging storm destroyed it in 1984. In 1889, a red sector was inserted in the light to mark Cross Rip Shoal and other shoals south of it and wrecks became less common. The current tower has solar panels built into the masonry and sits on a five foot thick concrete mat which protects the lighthouse from erosion. Great Point Light flashes white every 5 seconds.

© William Johnson

Brant Point Light

Brant Point Light claims several distinctions: it is the country's second oldest lighthouse (1746), after Boston Light (1716); it is the most offen rebuilt on the east coast (9 times); it is the lowest light in New England at 26 feet above sea level. The current tower, built in 1901, sits on the western side of Nantucket Harbor. Brant Point Light flashes red every 4 seconds and is visible 10 miles out to sea.

© William Johnson

Sankaty Head Light

Sankaty Head Light, built in 1850, this red and white striped light sits 158 feet above sea level and is visible 28 miles out to sea.Sankaty Head was originally fitted with a second-order lens, which was replaced in 1987 with a revolving airport beacon. It flashes a white light every 7.5 seconds. Sankaty Head is a commanding bluff some 90 feet above the sea on the east coast of Nantucket. Sankaty Head Light is in danger due to erosion.

© Terry Pommett

Boston and South Shore Lights

Scituate Light

Scituate Light, built in 1811, the 50 foot original granite tower stands today next to the keeper's quarters. This light, guarding the entrance to Scituate Harbor, is located midway between Plymouth and Boston. The light was taken out of service in 1890, replaced by the offshore light at Minot's Ledge. The light was reactivated in 1990 and owned by the town of Scituate

© Marjorie Monteleon

Minots Ledge Light

This light is known as the "I love you" light, named for its 1-4-3 flashing pattern. The original tower, first lit in 1860, was not strong enough to withstand huge tidal surges of a powerful storm. In April 1851 the light was swept into the sea, killing the two assistant keepers on duty. A new 114-foot lighthouse went into service in 1860. The light was automated in 1947 and converted to solar power in 1983.

© Paul Star

Graves Ledge Light

Graves Ledge Light, built on a rock ledge in 1905, this 113 foot granite block tower guides ships through the north channel into Boston's inner harbor. Originally fitted with a 1st-order Fresnel lens, the light is now automated and flashes twice every 12 seconds.

© Paul Star

Boston Light

This light built on Little Brewster Island in Boston Harbor in 1716 was America's first lighthouse. Ben Franklin wrote a "doggeral ditty" about the death by drowning of the first keeper, George Worthlake. The lighthouse suffered extensive damage during the Revolutionary War from the Americans and British, and was rebuilt in 1783. The tower was modified again in 1859. Boston Light's 98 foot tower flashes its 1.75 million candlepower beacon every 10 seconds, visible for 27 miles. The lighthouse is the last remaining manned station in the United States.

© Jim Abts

North Shore Lights

Guarding the entrance to Marblehead harbor, the current pyramidal skeleton light tower was erected in 1895. It replaced the original light tower built in 1836. This 105 foot-tall cast iron tower is the only one of its kind in New England. The light, now automated, has been recently restored. The light, at 130 feet above the harbor, shines a fixed green light.

© Jim Abts
© Courtney Thompson

Marblehead Light

Twin Lights

Located just offshore from Rockport, the twin lights of Cape Ann were established in 1771. The twin lights were the last of 12 Colonial era lights. Originally 45 feet tall, the towers were replaced in 1861 by the current 124 foot-tall granite towers. Both towers originally had 1st-order Fresnel lenses. The north tower was deactvated in 1932 and the south tower was automated. The north tower has recently been restored. Twin lights is commonly called Thatchers Island Light.

© Paul Star

Baker Island Light

Baker Island Light , established in 1789, guards the entrance to Salem harbor. The light station originally displayed two lights. The companion tower was deactivated in 1870. The current 59-foot tower is still in use. It alternates white and red flashes 7 seconds apart.

© Paul Star
© Courtney Thompson

Hospital Point Light

Hospital Point Light , constructed in 1872, the current light is located in the town of Beverly. This light tower guards the channel to Salem harbor. A beacon was installed in a church steeple that was located behind the light tower. This beacon is also currently active.

© Paul Star

Annisquam Light

Wigwam Point, at the entrance to Annisquam Harbor, first had a light in 1801. The current 41 foot tower replaced the original in 1897. The tower was first equipped with a fifth-order lens, upgraded to a fourth-order in 1922, and now fitted with a 1000 watt bulb. The flashing white light has a range of 14 nautical miles.

© Allen Karsh

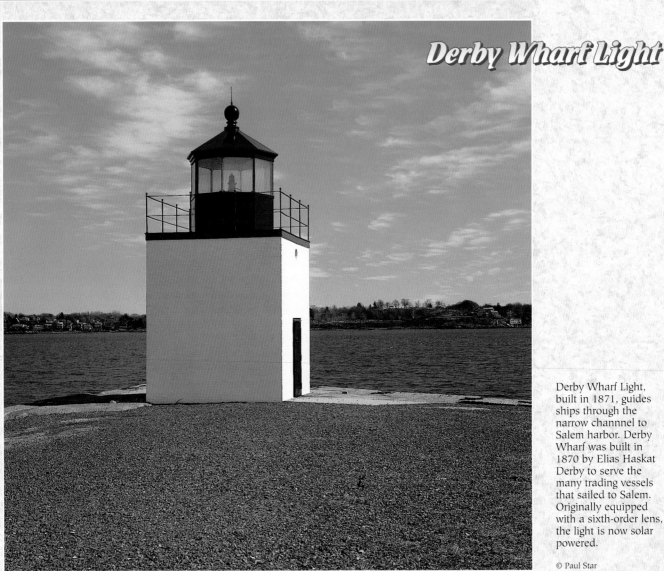

Derby Wharf Light

Derby Wharf Light, built in 1871, guides ships through the narrow channnel to Salem harbor. Derby Wharf was built in 1870 by Elias Haskat Derby to serve the many trading vessels that sailed to Salem. Originally equipped with a sixth-order lens, the light is now solar powered.

© Paul Star

Eastern Point Light

The first lighthouse at Eastern Point , guarding the eastern entrance to Gloucester Harbor, was built in 1832. The current tower replaced the original in 1890. This 36-foot white brick tower had a fourth-order lens, but now shines a beacon optic. The light was automated in 1986. In the 1880's artist Winslow Homer lived at Eastern Point.

© William Johnson

Plum Island Light

The harbor entrance on Plum Island, at the mouth of the Merrimac River, was the site for two range lights built in 1783. The towers have been rebuilt and relocated several times. The current and only remaining tower was rebuilt in 1898. Automated in 1981, the light has been restored by the Coast Guard.

© Paul Star

New Hampshire Lights

White Island Light, constructed in 1821, sits on one of the Isles of Shoals most barren outcroppings. The original stone tower was 82 feet tall. The current 58 foot tall brick tower dates back to 1859. Built to withstand the pounding surf, the walls are two feet thick. The light is now automated and solar powered.

© Tom Mitchell

White Island Light

Isles of Shoals

Isles of Shoals are located five miles off the coast of Portsmouth. These isles were home to one of the earliest European settlements in North America. In the sixteenth century many fishermen and families inhabited the Shoals' nine lands, in search of the abundant schools of fish in the North Atlantic.

© Jim Abts

Fort Point Light

This light is known by several other names: Fort Constitution Light, Newcastle Light , and Portsmouth Harbor Light. This site was one of the original Colonial towers, with a light dating from 1771. The current 48 foot cast iron tower was built in 1877. The light still shines through a fourth-order lens, with a flashing green light.

© Marjorie Monteleon

Whaleback Light

Whaleback Light, built in 1820, is located off the coast of Kittery Point, Maine, yet protects Portsmouth harbor. Both Maine and New Hampshire like to lay claim to Whaleback. The light is positioned closer to Maine. The current 72-foot tall unpainted granite tower was constructed in 1872 and fitted with a fourth-order lens. The white flashing light and foghorn are both automated.

© William Johnson

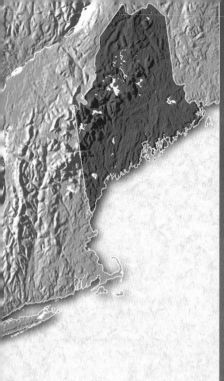

Maine Lights

Nubble Light

Nubble Light "Cape Neddick Light", built in 1879, is the southernmost light in Maine. Situated on a barren rock island "the Nubble" off Cape Neddick, this light is considered one of the most popular scenic attractions along the coast. The 41-foot cast iron tower is fitted with a fourth-order lens, flashing red every six seconds. Nubble's height above water is 88 feet with a range of 13 nautical miles.

© Dianne Dietrich Leis

Goat Island Light

Goat Island Light, built in 1822 and rebuilt in 1859, sits on the southwest end of Goat Island near the entrance to Cape Porpoise harbor. This light was Maine's last manned light station, not automated until 1990. Its height above water is 38 feet with a range of 12 nautical miles.

© Paul Star

Wood Island Light

Wood Island Light marks the entrance of the Saco River and lies just offshore from Biddeford Pool. This light, built in 1808 and rebuilt in 1858, sits on the east end of Wood Island. The light was automated in 1986. It s height above water is 71 feet above water and range is 24 miles.

© Paul Star

Cape Elizabeth Light

Cape Elizabeth Light "Two Lights", built in 1828, are located near Two Lights State Park. The west light was dismanteled in 1824 and now privately owned. The east tower, visible for 27 nautical miles, is the most powerful beacon on the New England coast, at four-million candle power. Two Lights height above water is 129 feet.
The Fresnel lens is now on display at the Cape Elizabeth Town Hall.

© Tom Mitchell

Spring Point Ledge Light

Spring Point Ledge Light was originally built in 1855 and rebuilt prior to 1897.This light is located offshore from Fort Preble, marking the west side of the main entrance to Portland Harbor. The present 40 foot caisson type concrete tower was built in 1897. First constructed as an offshore light, not until 1951 was it connected to the mainland by a 900-foot breakwater. The light was automated in 1934.

© Paul Star

Portland Head Light

The oldest lighthouse in Maine, Portland Head Light has guided maritime traffic through the entrance to Portland Harbor for over 200 years. Local merchants began petitioning the Massachusetts legislature for a lighthouse at Portland Head as early as 1784. A maritime tragedy in 1787 finally prompted the legislature to approve a small appropriation of $750.00 to begin construction of a 58 foot tower of rubblestone set in lime. The Lighthouse Act of 1789 transferred responsibility for aids to navigaton from the individual states to the Federal Government and in 1790 under the authorization from President George Washington, $1500.00 was appropriated for the completion of the lighthouse. Portland Head Light flickered into operation just before sunset on January 10, 1791. Portland Head Light is on the National Register of Historic Places.

© Jim Abts

Portland Breakwater Light

Portland Breakwater Light "Bug Light" was built in 1855, replaced in 1875, automated in 1934 and now inactive. The light underwent major renovation in 1990 and is listed on the National Register of Historic Places. The light, complete with its Corinthian Columns, was created to resemble a 4th century Greek monument.

© Tom Mitchell

Ram Island Ledge Light

Ram Island Ledge Light was built in 1905 to ease the cause of many shipwrecks that ran upon the ledge at high tide. The lighthouse was constructed of grey granite blocks, cut and transported from Vinalhaven .The light was automated in 1959. Located offshore from Fort Williams Park, Cape Elizabeth, its height above water is 77 feet and range is 12 nautical miles.

© Tom Mitchell

Seguin Light

The original 38 foot tower was built in 1875, by order of President George Washington at a cost of $6300.00. Located two miles south of the mouth of the Kennebec River, Seguin Light was Maine's second lighthouse. The light has been rebuilt twice, in 1820 and 1857. The present tower (1857) is 57 feet tall and at 186 feet above the water is the highest above water on the Maine coast. It can be seen at a distance of 40 miles. The tower accomodates Maine's only first-order lens. The light also has one of the most powerful foghorns made. The light was automated in 1985. The Coast Guard maintains the light. The island and keepers quarters are maintained by the Friends of Seguin Island, a non-profit organization. A small museum is located on the north side of the keepers house.

© Ron Monteleon

Hendrick's Head Light

Hendrick's Head Light, built in 1829, is on Southport Island on the east side of the mouth of the Sheepscot River. The current 39 foot-tall tower was built in 1875. The station, discontinued in 1933 and automated in 1951, is now privately owned. The property has been carefully and accurately restored by the current owners.

© Kevin Shields

Burnt Island Light

Burnt Island Light was built in 1821 and altered in 1888. Changes were made because its light interfered with the light from Cuckold's Light. Burnt Island Light is located on the west side entrance to Boothbay Harbor. Its height above water is 61 feet. The red and white light flashes with a range of red 12 nautical miles and white 15 nautical miles.

© Ron Monteleon

Cuckolds Light

Cuckolds Light, established as a fog signal station 1n 1892, had the light tower added in 1907. The light was automated in 1975. Cuckolds sits on a small island less than a mile from the tip of Southport Island and the village of Newagen. Its height above water is 59 feet with a range of 12 nautical miles.

© Marjorie Monteleon

Ram Island Light

Ram Island Light, built in 1883, this light is located on Ram Island off Ocean Point. This light guards the channel"Fishermans Passage". The light was automated in 1965 and after falling into disrepair, was rebuilt by the Coast Guard in 1977. Its height above water is 36 feet.

© Tom Mitchell

Pemaquid Point Light

Pemaquid Point Light, comissioned in 1827 by John Quincy Adams, this light is located on the west side of the entrance to Muscongus Bay. The lighthouse was rebuilt in 1857 and automated in 1934.The keeper's house is home for the "Fisherman's Museum, operated by the town of Bristol. Its height above water is 79 feet and the flashing white light ranges 14 nautical miles.

© David Ransaw

Marshall Point Light

Marshall Point Light, built in 1832 and rebuilt in 1857, marks the eastern boundary of Muscongus Bay and the entrance to Port Clyde Harbor. The light was automated in 1980 and the town of St. George acquired the keeper's house and grounds. The keeper's house was placed on the National Register of Historic Places in 1988. Restored by the St. George Historical Society, the keeper's house is now home for the Marshall Point Lighthouse Museum. The light's height above water is 30 feet and has a range of 13 nautical miles.

© Robert Dennis

Monhegan Light

Monhegan Island Light is located at the center of the island at the island's highest elevation. The lighthouse, at 178 feet above the water, is the second highest along the Maine Coast. The light was built in 1824 and rebuilt in 1850. Its flashing white light has a range of 21 nautical miles. The light was automated in 1959. The keeper's house is now a museum. Monhegan Island is 10 miles off the Maine Coast south of Port Clyde. Settled in 1614, the island represents Maine's earliest fishing village.

© Kevin Shields

Owls Head Light

Owls Head Light, built in 1825, guards the south entrance to Rockland Harbor. The light, only 20 feet tall, stands 100 feet above the water. Owls Head Light is on the National Register of Historic Places. The light has a range of 16 nautical miles.

© Jim Abts

Rockland Breakwater Light

Rockland Breakwater Light, built in 1888, is at the end of the 0.8 mile-long stone breakwater extending into Rockland Harbor from Jameson Point. Construction of the breakwater started in 1881 and was completed in 1889. The present light was constructed in 1902. The light was automated in 1964. The light's height above water is 39 feet, with a range of 17 nautical miles.

© Marjorie Monteleon

Browns Head Light

The light was originallly built in 1832 and rebuilt in 1857.The light is located on the northeast point of Vinalhaven Island, the entrance to Fox Island Thorofare. The fog bell tower was removed after automation in 1987. Brown's Head height above water is 39 feet.

© Kevin Shields

Heron Neck Light

The light is located on the southern tip of Green Island, just south of Carver's Harbor on Vinalhaven Island. Heron Neck was built in 1854 and guards the east entrance to Hurricane Sound. A fire nearly destroyed the keeper's house in 1989: however the property has been completely restored. The light's height above water is 92 feet.

© Marjorie Monteleon

Matinicus Rock Light

The light is located on a barren 30 acre rock island five miles southeast of Matinicus Island.This lighthouse, located on the south side of "the Rock", is perhaps the most isolated light station on the Maine coast. Twin wooden towers were first built in 1827 and replaced with granite towers in 1848. Both towers were rebuilt in 1857. The light was automated in 1833. "The Rock" is also a nesting area for various seabirds, including the Atlantic Puffin. The light's height above water is 90 feet, with a range of 20 nautical miles.

© Marjorie Monteleon

Curtis Island Light

Curtis Island Light, built in 1836 and rebuilt in 1896, is on the south side entrance to Camden Harbor. This five acre island is named after Cyris Curtis, founder of the Saturday Evening Post. This light has a fixed beacon which is 52 feet above water, with a range of 6 nautical miles. The light was automated in 1972 and deeded to the town of Camden.

© Andy Payson

Grindel Point Light

Grindel Point Light, built in 1851, guards the north side entrance to Gilkey Harbor on Islesboro Island. The present square brick tower was constructed in 1874. The light was deactivated in 1934 and given to the town of Islesboro. The light was recommisioned in 1987 and is now solar powered. The Islesboro Sailors Memorial Museum is located in the Keeper's House.The fog bell on the southside of the light tower is on loan from the Shore Village Museum in Rockland, Maine. The lights height above water is 39 feet, with a range of 6 nautical miles.

© Tom Mitchell

Dyce's Head Light

The light was constructed in 1829 and remodeled in 1858. The keeper's house was again rebuilt in 1937. The entire property is owned and mantained by the town of Castine. The light guards the north side entrance to Castine harbor. Castine, because of it's strategic location, has been occupied by the British, French, and Dutch. Thus having flown the flags of four nations

© Ron Monteleon

Eagle Island Light

Eagle Island Light, built in 1839 and rebuilt in 1858, sits on a bluff at the northeast end of Eagle Island. This 260 acre island lies halfway between Deer Isle and North Haven. The light was automated in 1959 and in 1963 the keeper's house was burned and other structures on the property demolished. The light and bell tower were saved. The light is now being restored. Its height above water is 106 feet ,with a range of 9 nautical miles.

© Marjorie Monteleon

Isle au Haut Light

Isle au Haut,named high island by French explorer Samuel de Champlain in 1604, is located six miles south of Stonington. The island is part of Acadia National Park. The lighthouse, located on Robinson Point , was built in 1907. The light was automated in 1934 and the property (except the tower) was sold at auction. The tower is still maintained by the Coast Guard. The keeper's house, now operated as a bed and breakfast, is on the National Register of Historic Places. The light's height above water is 48 feet.

© Marjorie Monteleon

The lighthouse is located on the southwest point of Mt. Desert, marking the entrance to Blue Hill Bay and Bass Harbor. The light was built in 1858 to assist ships seeking shelter in the harbor. The 32 foot tall brick tower is now automated, with a occulating red light Its height above water is 56 feet, with a range of 13 nautical miles.

© David Ransaw

This light,built in 1850 and rebuilt in 1891, marks the east side entrance to the inner harbor. The property is now part of an active military base.The light was automated in 1934. The light's height above water is 42 feet.

© David Ransaw

Prospect Harbor Light

West Quoddy Head Light

Located on the easternmost point of the continental United
States, this red and white striped lighthouse marks the southwest
entrance to Quoddy Channel. The light was originally built in
1807, under the orders of Thomas Jefferson, then rebuilt in 1858.
The light's height above water is 83 feet, with a range of 18
nautical miles.

© John Penrod

Petit Manan Lighthouse

Established in 1817 and rebuilt of granite in 1855, this is the second tallest lighthouse in Maine. The current
tower stands 119 feet tall and is located on the east point of Petit Manan Island, 2 1/2 miles off Petit Manan
Point in South Milbridge. The station also is equipped with a fog signal. This location is engulfed in fog nearly
20% of the time. Its height is 123 feet above the water, with a range of 26 nautical miles.

© Ron Monteleon

Mulholland Light

The light is located on the east side of Lubec Channel on Campobello Island.This is a non-functioning light.

© Andy Payson

East Quoddy Head Light

This light is located on the northern end of Campobello Island, New Brunswick.The light is maintained by the Canadian Coast Guard.
The large red and white cross, typical of Canadian Lights, is intended to make visibility against a snowy background.This light is also called "Head Harbor Light".

© Andy Payson

Pub. by MEDS MAPS, Inc.
1 Walton Road - Harwich, MA 02645
Printed in Italy